The Castle in the Attic

Elizabeth Winthrop

TEACHER GUIDE

NOTE:
The trade book edition of the novel used to prepare this guide is found in the Novel Units catalog and on the Novel Units website. Using other editions may have varied page references.

Please note: We have assigned Interest Levels based on our knowledge of the themes and ideas of the books included in the Novel Units sets, however, please assess the appropriateness of this novel or trade book for the age level and maturity of your students prior to reading with them. You know your students best!

ISBN 978-1-56137-371-0

opyright infringement is a violation of Federal Law.

2020 by Novel Units, Inc., St. Louis, MO. All rights reserved. No part of is publication may be reproduced, translated, stored in a retrieval system, or ansmitted in any way or by any means (electronic, mechanical, photocopying, cording, or otherwise) without prior written permission from Novel Units, Inc.

eproduction of any part of this publication for an entire school or for a school stem, by for-profit institutions and tutoring centers, or for commercial sale is rictly prohibited.

ovel Units is a registered trademark of Conn Education.

inted in the United States of America.

To order, contact your local school supply store, or:

Toll-Free Fax: 877.716.7272
Phone: 888.650.4224
3901 Union Blvd., Suite 155
St. Louis, MO 63115

sales@novelunits.com

novelunits.com

Table of Contents

Summary 3

Introductory Activities 10

Chapter-by-Chapter 13
   Chapters contain: Vocabulary Words,
   Discussion Questions, Supplementary
   Activities, Predictions

Post-reading Activities 34

Bulletin Board Ideas 34

Journal Prompts 35

Vocabulary Activities 35

Teacher Background 38

Bibliography 39

Assessment 40

Skills and Strategies

Thinking
Evaluating, visualization, synthesis

Literary Elements
Fantasy as a genre, story elements, characterization

Vocabulary
Synonyms/antonyms, thesaurus, analogies, categorize, word mapping

Comprehension
Predicting, comparison/contrast

Writing
Newspaper article, exposition, narrative, journaling

Listening/Speaking
Interviewing, role play, mood, news bite

Summary of *The Castle in the Attic*

William is an imaginative ten-year-old who competes in gymnastics, relates easily to his physician mother and architect father, and is "coping" (barely) with his nanny's decision to return to her home in England. Mrs. Phillips, the nanny, gives William a very special good-bye gift, an enormous stone and wooden castle which she had played with when she was a child. Mrs. Phillips explains to William that he is worthy of the castle because he is the "right person for it"; he has the "kind of gentle soul that accepts the rules of chivalry." While playing with the castle, William awakens the Silver Knight, who had been under one of Alastor's spells and was a small metal knight. Alastor had been a wizard in the Silver Knight's father's court. William enters the magical world and size of the Silver Knight and defeats the evil wizard in a mythical quest.

Using Predictions

We all make predictions as we read—little guesses about what will happen next, how the conflict will be resolved, which details given by the author will be important to the plot, which details will help to fill in our sense of a character. Students should be encouraged to predict, to make sensible guesses. As students work on predictions, these discussion questions can be used to guide them: What are some of the ways to predict? What is the process of a sophisticated reader's thinking and predicting? What clues does an author give us to help us in making our predictions? Why are some predictions more likely than others?

A predicting chart is for students to record their predictions. As each subsequent chapter is discussed, you can review and correct previous predictions. This procedure serves to focus on predictions and to review the stories.

- Use the facts and ideas the author gives.
- Use your own knowledge.
- Use new information that may cause you to change your mind.

Predictions:
_____
_____
_____
_____

Prediction Chart

What characters have we met so far?	What is the conflict in the story?	What are your predictions?	Why did you make those predictions?

Story Map

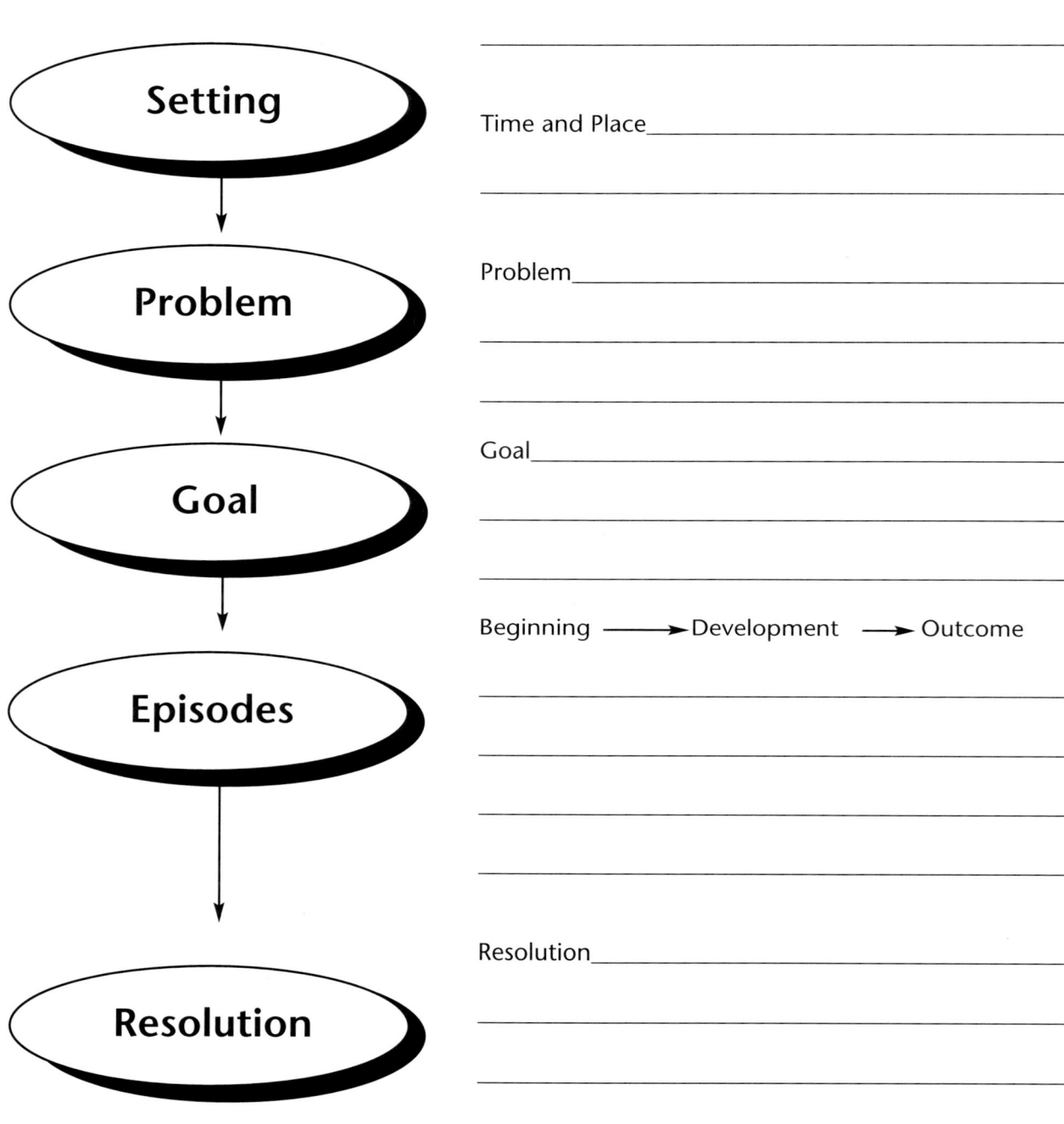

Characters _____
_____
_____

Time and Place _____
_____
_____

Problem _____
_____
_____
_____

Goal _____
_____
_____

Beginning ⟶ Development ⟶ Outcome
_____
_____
_____
_____
_____
_____

Resolution _____
_____
_____
_____

Using Character Webs

Attribute Webs are simply a visual representation of a character from the novel. They provide a systematic way for the students to organize and recap the information they have about a particular character. Attribute webs may be used after reading the novel to recapitulate information about a particular character or completed gradually as information unfolds, done individually, or finished as a group project.

One type of character attribute web uses these divisions:
- How a character acts and feels. (How does the character feel in this picture? How would you feel if this happened to you? How do you think the character feels?)
- How a character looks. (Close your eyes and picture the character. Describe him to me.)
- Where a character lives. (Where and when does the character live?)
- How others feel about the character. (How does another specific character feel about our character?)

In group discussion about the student attribute webs and specific characters, the teacher can ask for backup proof from the novel. You can also include inferential thinking.

Attribute webs need not be confined to characters. They may also be used to organize information about a concept, object or place.

Attribute Web

The attribute web below is designed to help you gather clues the author provides about what a character is like. Fill in the blanks with words and phrases which tell how the character acts and looks, as well as what the character says and what others say about him or her.

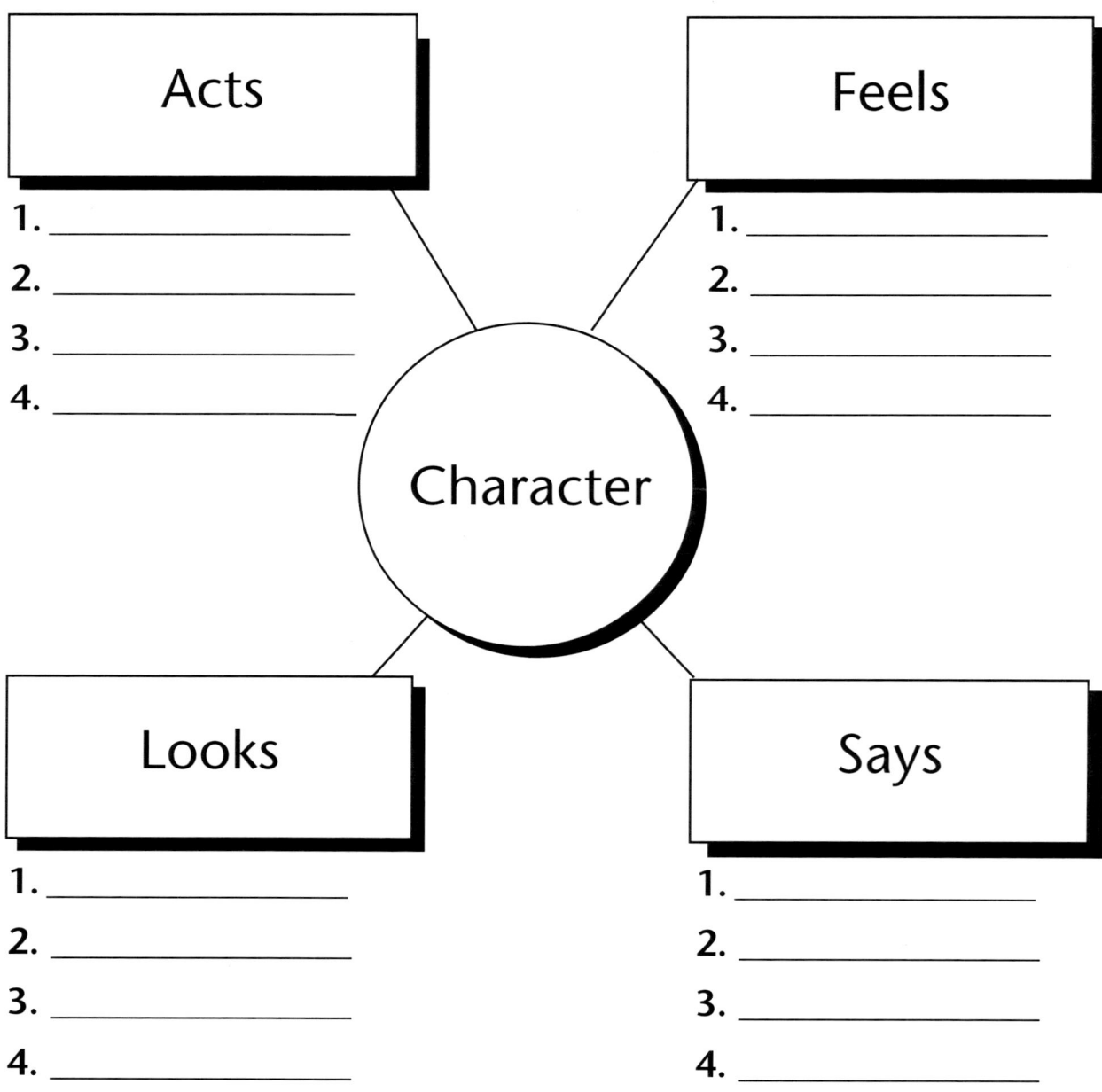

Acts
1. _____
2. _____
3. _____
4. _____

Feels
1. _____
2. _____
3. _____
4. _____

Looks
1. _____
2. _____
3. _____
4. _____

Says
1. _____
2. _____
3. _____
4. _____

© Novel Units, Inc.   All rights reserved

Attribute Web

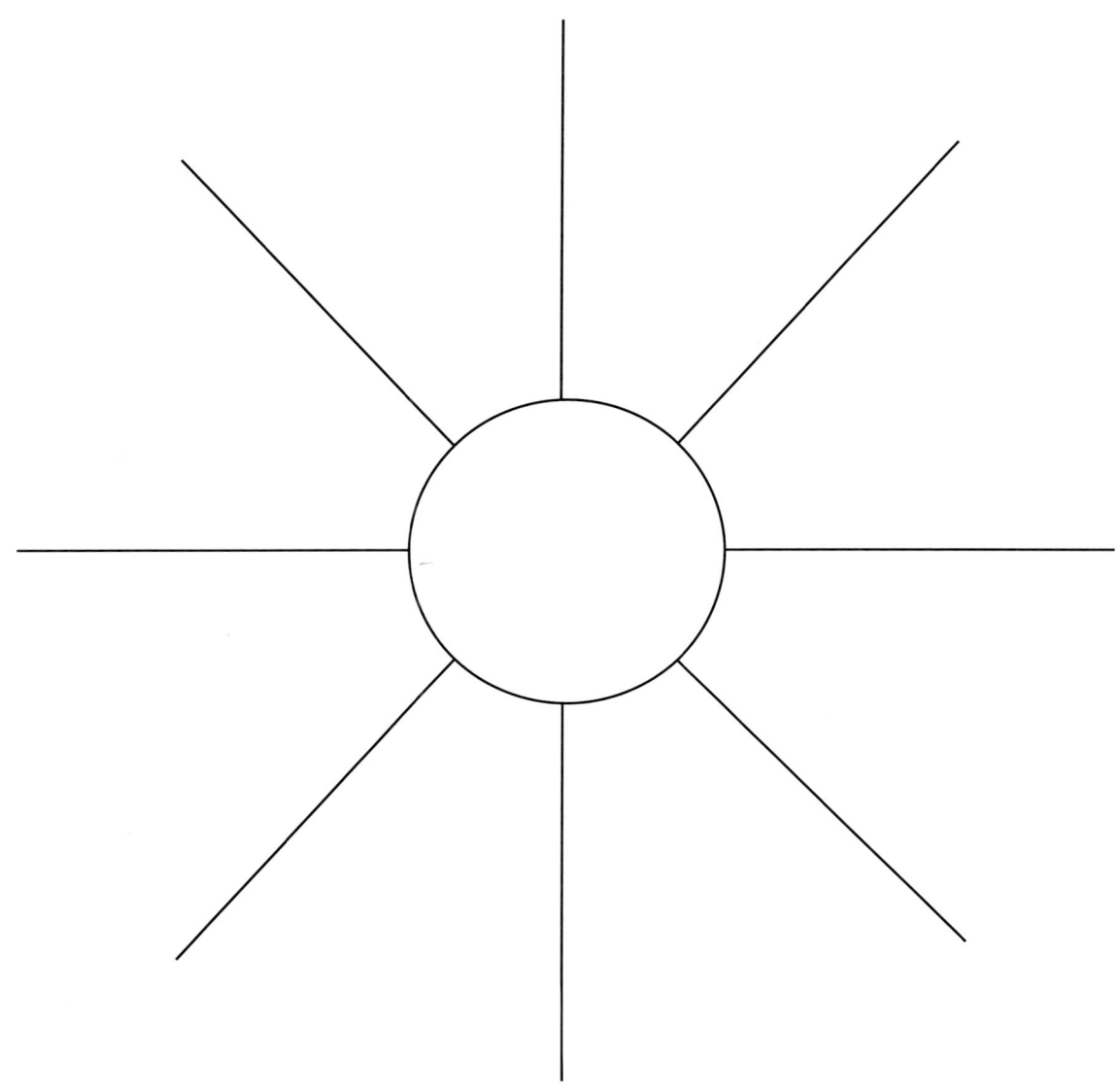

Initiating Activities

1. Brainstorm the word "Fantasy."

2. This book involves a quest. What do you expect? (A quest is a search or pursuit made in order to find or obtain something.) Make some predictions.

3. Thumb through the book. Look at the cover and end papers. Make some predictions about the book.

4. Put on your collection librarian's hat. Read the reviews of the book. What do you expect? Justify your answers.

   - "The adventure William encounters in the fantasy world is intense, and his face-off with the wizard is satisfyingly dramatic."

   - "Winthrop has the real gift for fantasy, creating a believable imaginary world that nevertheless relates to the real world. William's attic castle is also the castle of William himself."

   - "A satisfying quest fantasy...will appeal to a wide range of readers."

   - "Large-size magic...the charms are unfailing."

5. Get ready to meet a new friend—William who competes in gymnastics, is an only child, has parents who are a physician and an architect, and is ten years old. Make some predictions about a book with William as the main character.

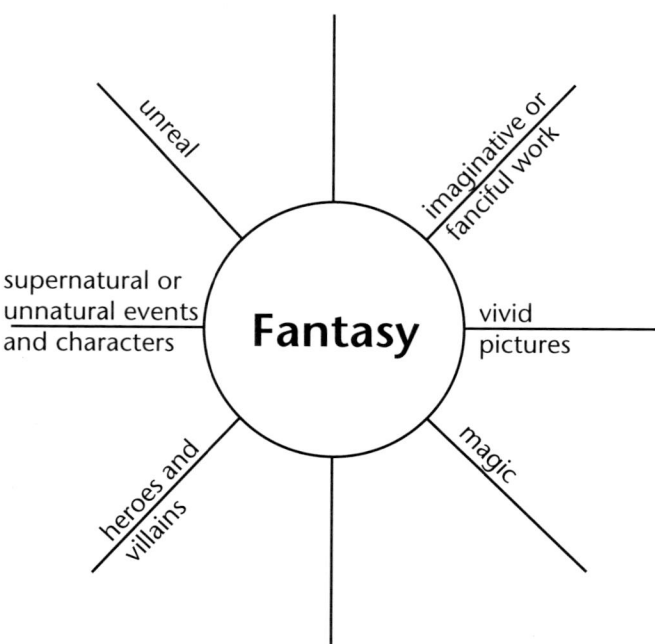

A Coat of Arms for William

Directions: Decide which elements about William should be included on a coat of arms. Using color, illustration, and words, complete the coat of arms pattern below.

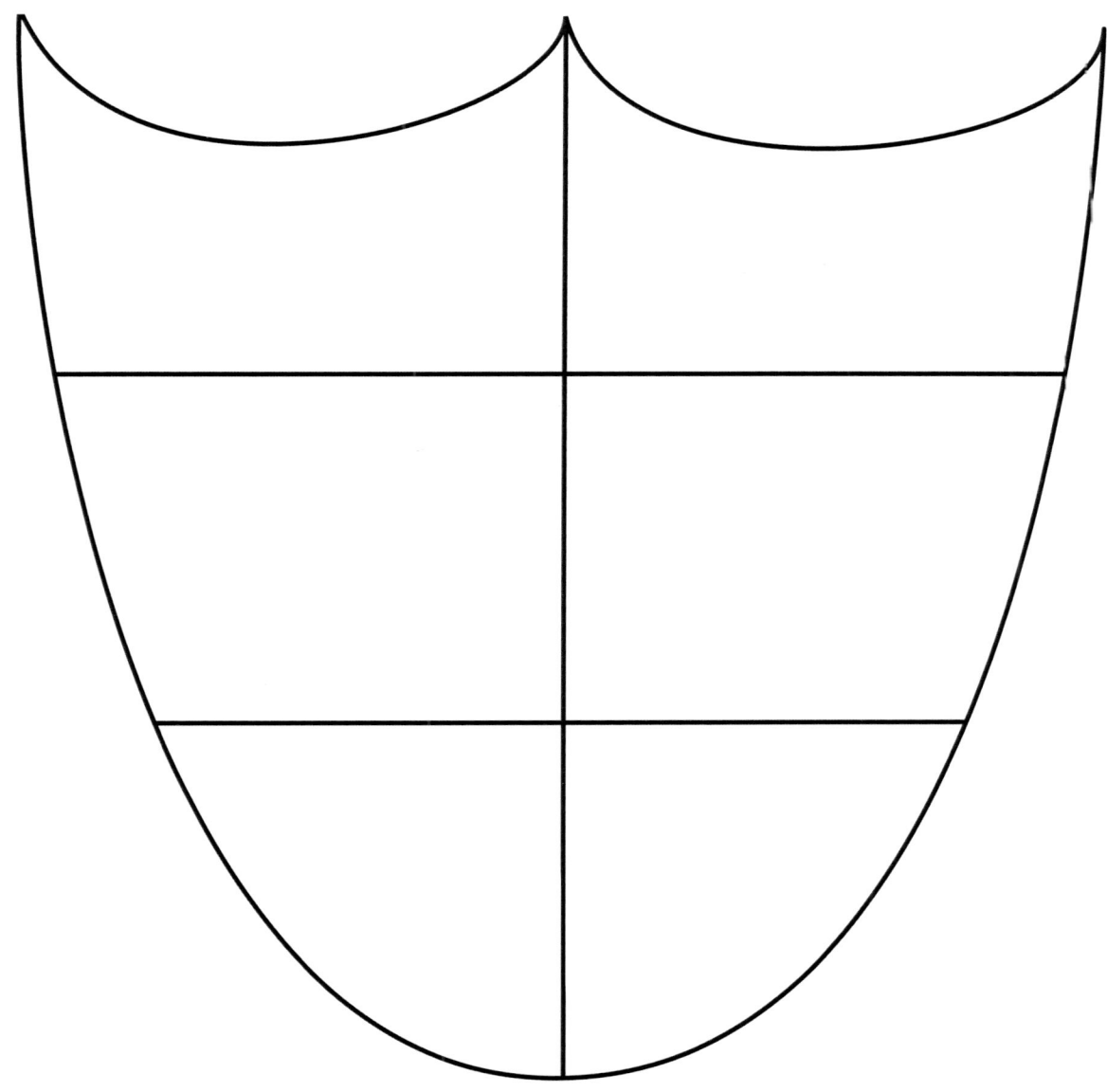

A T-Shirt for William

Directions: Design a t-shirt for William. On the bottom of this sheet explain why it is appropriate.

_____
_____
_____
_____.

Chapter-by-Chapter
Vocabulary, Discussion Questions, and Activities

Chapter 1   Pages 3-7

Vocabulary
> bureau 6

Discussion Questions
1. How would William characterize the Monday in Chapter 1? *(Answers vary: "downer," "the pits," "sad.")* Why? *(Several things went wrong for him. He couldn't master an Arabian dive roll in his gymnastics routine. Mrs. Phillips told him she plans to return to England. It was raining.)*

2. Is William at age ten able to take care of himself? *(Answers vary. Students may organize responses in a chart with columns labeled "yes" and "no.")*

3. What is the significance of Mrs. Phillips' pearl circle pin and picture of her husband? *(The items are Mrs. Phillips' most prized possessions. William hides the objects in an attempt to keep Mrs. Phillips with his family.)* What kind of thinking led William to such actions? *(immature, childish, self-centered, concern for immediate answers, simplistic)*

4. Why didn't Mrs. Phillips ask William directly about her missing keepsakes? *(Answers vary. She didn't want to embarrass him.)*

5. What do you think of the way William's mother handled the missing objects? *(Answers vary.)*

6. What does Mrs. Phillips mean that William has a "gentle heart"? *(Answers vary. He is kind and thoughtful and sensitive.)*

Prediction
What will the surprise be?

Supplementary Activities
1. Interview some adults and students about whether a ten-year-old can take care of himself after school. Report your answers orally and prepare a class graphing of the results.

2. What would you name as your two most prized possessions? How are your selections similar to or different from Mrs. Phillips'?

Chapter 2   Pages 8-16

Vocabulary

chivalry 9	entrusted 9	drawbridge 10	portcullis 10
armory 11	buttery 11	scullery 11	troubadours 11
jesters 11	minstrels 12	wardrobe 12	allure 12

Discussion Questions

1. Why does William look "like a horse at the starting gate" at the beginning of Chapter 2? *(He was anxious to see the surprise Mrs. Phillips had for him.)* What kind of a descriptive device did the author use here? *(a simile)* Why are similes useful? *(They give the reader visual images.)*

2. What is the surprise? *(an enormous stone and wooden castle which had been Mrs. Phillips' when she was a child)*

3. What are rules of chivalry? *(Teachers: Look to page 98 in the book where the rules of chivalry are detailed in the fourth paragraph.)* Why do you think they are important to Mrs. Phillips? *(Answers vary.)*

4. Using the diagram of the castle, conduct a tour for a partner. Be sure to use the correct terms.

5. What does Mrs. Phillips remember of the legend of the Silver Knight? *(The knight was long ago thrown out of his kingdom by an enemy and one day he'll come back to life and reclaim his land.)*

6. What are William's feelings as he and Mrs. Phillips eat dinner in Chapter 2? *(sad, unsettled)* Have you ever had something "hang" between you and someone else? Share your feelings.

7. Why is Mrs. Phillips' leaving? *(Answers vary, but include notion that William will be closer to his parents with her gone.)*

8. Look at these castle terms. Look for modern-day equivalents or near equivalents.

Castle-times	Modern Day
Drawbridge	Bridge
Portcullis	Gate
Armory	Bulletproof vest
Buttery	Pantry/refrigerator
Scullery	Kitchen
Troubadours	Singers/entertainers
Jesters	Clowns/entertainers
Wardrobe	Closet
Allure	Hall

© Novel Units, Inc.   All rights reserved

Supplementary Activities

1. Locate a copy of *King Arthur and the Knights of the Round Table* so you can read a couple of chapters.

2. What is Marmite? Check at specialty food stores or with someone from England to answer. Try tasting it, if you can.

3. Speculate about what happened to the other soldiers in the castle. Write a short paragraph to explain your answer.

4. Interview a parent or older sibling about family traditions. Fill in a class web to record answers.

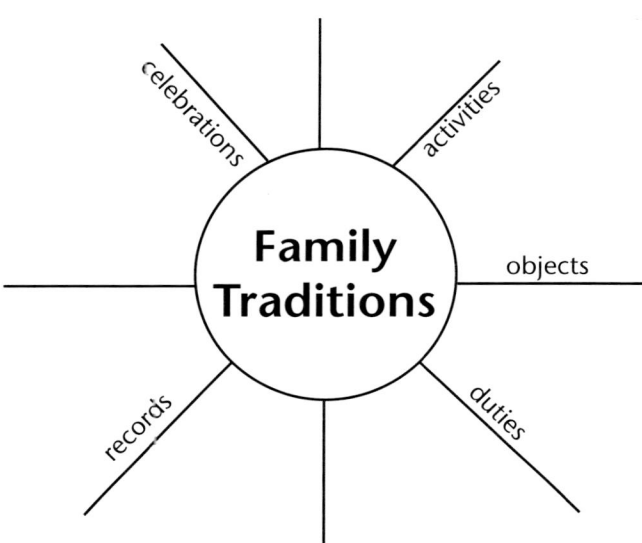

Chapter 3 Pages 17-25

Vocabulary

gnawed 17   loomed 18   scabbard 19   plume 20
shinguards 22

Discussion Questions

1. Who is Bear? *(William's stuffed animal)* What is so special about stuffed animals that many children cherish them? *(Answers vary.)* Is William at ten too old for a stuffed animal? *(Answers vary.)*

2. Why does William take Bear with him to the attic? *(feeling of protection and safety)*

3. On page 19, the author mentions an "odd, expectant feeling" in the attic. What does that mean? How would a movie director create such a feeling? Why does the author dwell on the feeling? *(to build suspense and expectation and because meeting the knight is very significant in the story)*

4. Why does William drop the knight? *(The knight is soft and warm and alive and that fact amazes and scares William.)*

5. What does William learn about the Silver Knight in his first meeting? *(The Silver Knight is about the size of William's index finger, is a soldier, is puzzled and curious about William, acts human, talks of magic, and tokens, and spells.)*

Prediction

How is this book shaping up? How will the medal figure in the rest of the book?

Supplementary Activities

1. Draw a picture of the medal. Where have you seen something similar? *(at the beginning of each chapter)*

2. Start an attribute web recording information and impressions of William. Provide support from the book for your descriptions. (See next page.)

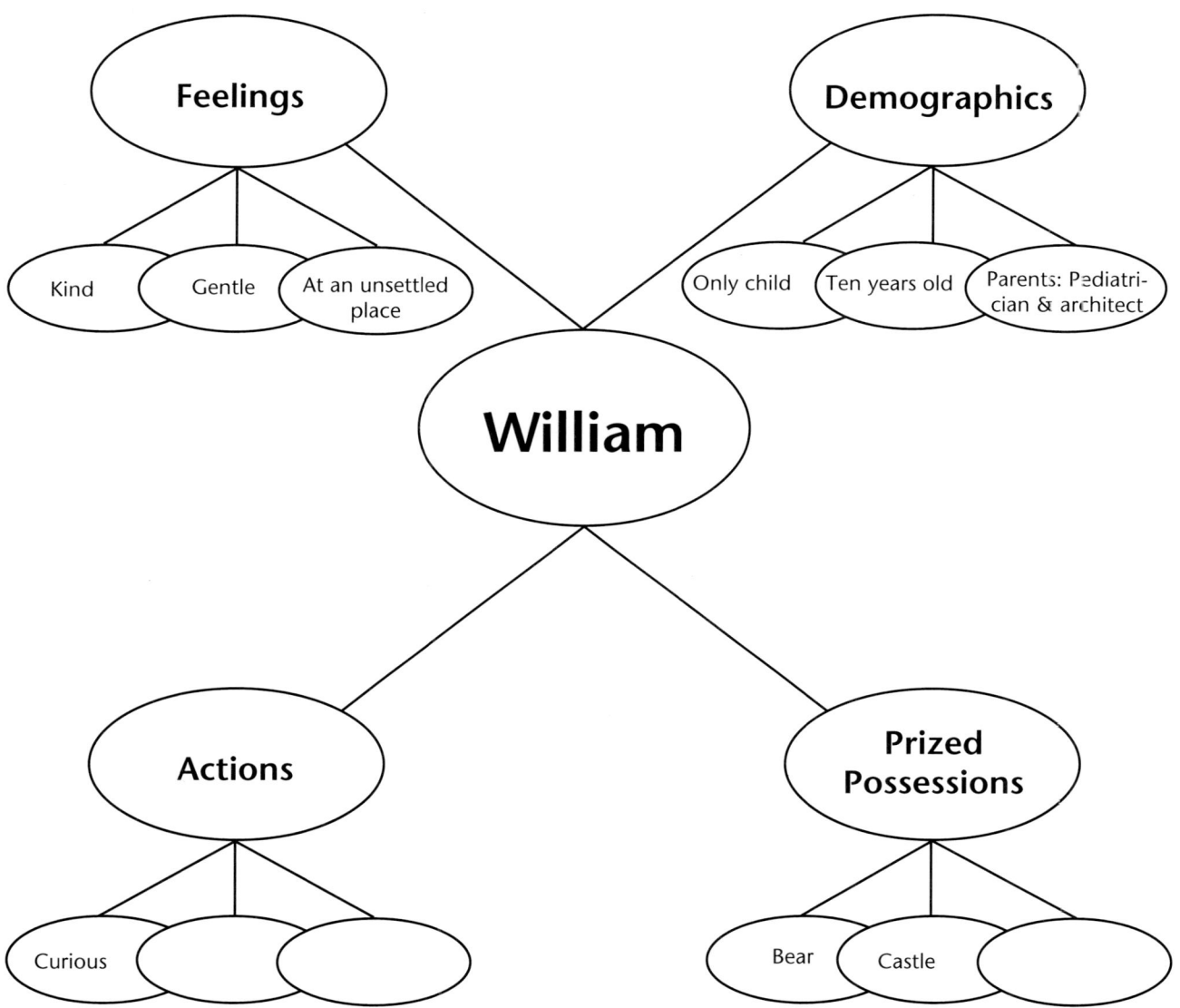

Chapter 4   Pages 26-40

Vocabulary

scrounge 27	topography 27	brunt 28	reckoned 31
battlements 31	raggle-taggle 33	garbled 33	secretive 34
mystified 35	palsy 35	councillors 35	edicts 36

Discussion Questions

1. What one or two words would you use to describe William's relationship with his parents? *(Answers vary; interested, inquiring.)*

2. Why did William and Jason become friends? *(They were both out-of-the-ordinary in looks, and so banded together.)* How do you make friends? What people do you choose as friends?

3. Why didn't William invite Jason over to see the castle? *(William was concerned about keeping the Silver Knight hidden. Perhaps he wanted to keep the castle and knight to himself.)*

4. What is the knight's story? *(pages 32-38)*

5. Why did William offer to bring the Silver Knight a bug? *(to test the medal)*

6. Identify Janus. (See page 38 of this guide.) Why is this Greek mythological figure important to the story?

Supplementary Activities

1. Alastor poisoned the Silver Knight's father's mind. What things would you say to do that? Discuss with a classmate and then write a short paragraph to answer.

2. Make a list of questions to ask the Silver Knight. Have a classmate take the part and conduct an interview.

Chapter 5   Pages 41-48

Vocabulary
    vaulted 45   rummaged 46

Discussion Questions
1. What problems does William encounter since breaking the spell and bringing the Silver Knight to life? *(providing food for the knight, keeping the knight a secret)*

2. Who is Jason? *(William's best friend)* Pick three adjectives to describe Jason. Give a reason and evidence from the book for each of your choices. *(Answers vary.)*

3. What do you think of William's gymnastics coach? *(Answers vary.)* How does he compare to any coaches you've known? *(Answers vary.)*

4. Why doesn't William share the Silver Knight with Jason? *(Answers vary. He wants to keep the knight special. He is afraid of ridicule or trouble.)*

5. What is the close call when William's father looks over the castle? *(William's father looks in the stable where Sir Simon is hiding and actually picks up his shield.)*

6. How does Mr. Lawrence react to the castle? *(He's enthusiastic and decides to build a moat to add to the castle's defenses.)*

7. Start an attribute web for Mr. Lawrence. *(Architect; Enthusiastic at the start of projects but often didn't finish; Generally responsible parent)*

Supplementary Activities
1. Compare you and your family to William's family. *(Students may organize ideas in a chart to include comparisons of occupations, hobbies, and dispositions.)*

2. Consider what would surprise Sir Simon most about today's world. Write a short paragraph to answer.

3. Draw a cartoon panel to summarize the action in Chapter 5.

Chapter 6   Pages 49-56

Vocabulary

venison 51	tankard 51	ale 51	medallion 51
leer 51	squeamish 52	armory 53	ply 53
spit 55	portcullis 56	moat 56	

Discussion Questions

1. What does Sir Simon proclaim a miracle in Chapter 6? *(electricity and electric lights)* What other modern inventions would be miracles to Sir Simon? *(Answers vary.)*

2. Why is Janus an appropriate figure on the medallion?

3. How does Sir Simon find the word that makes the medallion work? *(reasonable guess)*

4. What do the words on the medallion mean? Predict. *(Answers vary.)*

5. Why does William seem uneasy in this chapter? *(He has been forced into telling lies and he's uncomfortable. He's uneasy about the future without Mrs. Phillips.)*

Supplementary Activities

1. Design a meal for the knight. Provide a scale model drawing of the meal. Remember the knight is about the size of William's index finger.

2. Choose one of these sayings to explain how it could relate to this chapter:

   - Having great potential is a burden.

   - Practice makes perfect.

3. Write a short paragraph starting with this sentence:

   William is blaming his shortcomings and problems on Mrs. Phillips because...

© Novel Units, Inc.   All rights reserved

Chapter 7 Pages 57-70

Vocabulary

spit 58	round-off 59	unobstructed 59
straddle presses 59-60	flip-flops 60	pursed 61
meddle 63	allotted 63	

Discussion Questions

1. How was it possible "the image of the token nibbled around the edges of William's mind for a couple of days"? *(Page 57, The image kept coming back to William, as though it were in the back of his mind and came to mind often.)* Have you ever had anything nibble around the edges of your mind? Why did the author choose the word "nibble" in this instance?

2. What were Sir Simon's ingenious mouse-preparing techniques? *(First he shrank the mouse with the medallion, then cooked it over a fire on a spit.)*

3. What precautions did William provide for Sir Simon's cooking? *(water in a small mustard jar and a toothpaste cup for scooping ashes, etc.)* What dangers did a live miniature knight bring? *(Answers vary.)*

4. Why was William's gymnastics workout so successful? *(William said it was his trying so hard because Mrs. Phillips was watching. She said it was William's concentration.)* What is your opinion? Support your answer with evidence from your own experiences.

5. Who was just the right lady for Sir Simon and what was William's idea? *(Mrs. Phillips; William planned to use the medallion to shrink Mrs. Phillips and put her into the castle.)*

6. Explain these things Mrs. Phillips said to William as she prepared to leave:

    Page 65, "I'm not really leaving, you know. I will always be with you in spirit."

    Page 66, "Don't you see I can't turn back now?"

    Page 67, "Certain places you must never return to."

    (Answers vary.)

7. How did William keep Mrs. Phillips from leaving? *(He used the medallion to shrink her.)*

Prediction

On page 63 Sir Simon warns that "there is a price to be paid when you meddle with a person's allotted time." What will happen because William has meddled?

Supplementary Activities
1. Identify these objects in Chapter 7—matches, silly bishops, green wooden box, belt pack, cat.
2. Discuss and answer in a short paragraph: What if the cat had caught Mrs. Phillips?
3. Sir Simon went to school only two mornings a week. What do you think he might have studied? Why?
4. Bring a chess board to the classroom to try out the game.
5. Write a short newspaper article describing Mrs. Phillips' shrinking.

Chapter 8   Pages 71-77

Vocabulary
resigned 74	repertoire 75	currant 75	wok 76
distracted 76			

Discussion Questions
1. What was William's hesitancy at the beginning of Chapter 8? *(He wasn't ready to face Mrs. Phillips because he had used magic to keep her near him. He hadn't asked her about the medallion first.)* How would you feel if you were William? Mrs. Phillips? Sir Simon?

2. Why did Sir Simon snap at William on page 72? *(He had discovered that William had explained nothing to Mrs. Phillips before shrinking her.)*

3. Explain William's thoughts as Sir Simon gave Mrs. Phillips a tour of the castle. *(oddly lonely)*

4. Why couldn't William explain his reasons to Mrs. Phillips? *(She wouldn't speak to him until he restored her to her normal size.)*

5. Why did William's dad come home a little early in Chapter 8? *(He knew Mrs. Phillips had gone and realized he had increased responsibilities.)*

6. What changes did Mr. Lawrence explain to William? *(Mr. Lawrence would try to get home earlier when Dr. Lawrence had evening hours so they could eat together.)* Do you think Mrs. Phillips planned for these changes?

7. Why is Mr. Lawrence easily distracted? *(Answers vary.)* How did William adjust to this trait in his father? *(Quiet acceptance; William also reminded his father of promises and expectations.)*

8. Why did the author mention William's stuffed bear at the end of Chapter 8? *(William needed comfort and the bear provided it.)*

Supplementary Activities

1. Change is a theme in this book. Discuss in a short paragraph.

2. Complete a story map for the first eight chapters of the book. (See page 6 of this guide.) Why does there seem to be a turning point in the book here?

3. Who was Vivaldi? Locate a recording and play it for your classmates.

Chapter 9   Pages 78-92

Vocabulary

inevitable 78	hasty 80	squire 80	quest 80
desperately 81	lame 83	deteriorating 83	notch 85
sheepishly 86	legacy 86	kindling 87	contraption 87
intricate 91	chiseled 91		

Discussion Questions

1. What problems did the characters have at the start of Chapter 9? How did they show their feelings?

Character	Problem	How Shown
William	Unsure how to proceed after shrinking Mrs. Phillips	Tried to make castle more comfortable
Mrs. Phillips	Captive in a child's castle	Not eating well, pacing at night
Sir Simon	Banished from kingdom by evil wizard Alastor	Works out, preparing to return and defeat wizard

2. Why didn't William's improvements in the castle win Mrs. Phillips over? *(She was so offended that William had shrunk her that she refused to speak to him until he made some efforts to restore her to her proper place and size.)*

3. Should William have shrunk Mrs. Phillips? *(Answers vary.)*

4. How did this saying relate to the story, "haste makes waste"? *(On page 80, William and Sir Simon considered that their use of the medallion to shrink Mrs. Phillips was an action taken in haste. Now they couldn't reverse their actions.)*

5. What did the riddle mean? *(Mrs. Phillips did needlework and Sir Simon practiced with his sword. Then the "squire" would cross the drawbridge and the time would be ready for the quest.)* Who was the squire? What was the quest?

6. Why did William desperately need to talk to Jason? *(William was uncertain about what to do and was scared.)* Have you ever needed to talk to someone desperately? How did you feel?

7. Look at the moat construction from different viewpoints.

   Father: *He is happy to be sharing something with his son; thinks he's helping; is pleased to finish a project.*

   William: *He is concerned lest his father discover the Silver Knight and Mrs. Phillips, and surprised that his father finished the moat.*

   Sir Simon: *He is unsettled being jostled about while the moat was installed.*

8. What decision did William make at the end of Chapter 9? *(to be shrunk and join those in the castle, hoping to regain the other half of the medallion and restore Mrs. Phillips and himself to their world)*

Prediction
What happens in the second half of the book?

Supplementary Activities
1. Writing: What would you advise William to take with him into the castle journey?

2. Why is Chapter 9 a turning point in the novel?

3. Have you ever experienced or heard about an unfinished parent project? Share with classmates. Why are such stories and experiences common?

4. Why are riddles and puzzles fun? Write a short paragraph to answer.

Chapter 10 Pages 93-107

Vocabulary

hoisted 93	courageous 93	intricately 94	surcoat 96
tunic 96	earnest 97	incantation 97	scabbard 98
midday 99	wanes 99	firescreen 103	pallet 104
drafty 104	incense 105	chain-mail 105	

Discussion Questions

1. Reread the first two paragraphs of Chapter 10. What clues do you find to the rest of the book? *(William will act as a soldier alongside Sir Simon. Courage will be important.)*

2. What things surprised William about the castle and being small? *(His voice sounded normal. The castle was very complete.)*

3. How did William learn the rules of chivalry? *(Sir Simon repeated the rules of conduct when he gave William his squire outfit.)*

4. How was William's training organized? *(In the morning, Sir Simon taught him about the use of his weapons and how to assist him. In the afternoon, he and Mrs. Phillips played chess and backgammon. He practiced his recorder and his gymnastics routines.)* How will his training help him? *(Answers vary.)*

5. What did Mrs. Phillips believe William would need to defeat the wizard? *(page 101, his brain, his footwork, and the sense of space he had developed as a gymnast)* How do you think these factors would affect William's success? *(Answers vary.)*

6. Before William declared that he was ready to go, he asked a lot of questions. Why? Did he have the answers before he was ready for the quest? *(no)* How, then, can he be ready? *(He believed in himself and believed he would have the answers and the necessary strength for whatever happened.)*

7. Why didn't William take Bear with him on his quest? *(Answers vary.)*

8. Why did Sir Simon fast and pray all night? *(It was the way of the knight. He wanted God's support in the quest.)*

Supplementary Activities

1. Look over the rules of chivalry on page 98. Evaluate them for today's world. Rewrite the rules of chivalry in today's language.

2. Locate a backgammon game to play at school.

3. Draw a picture of Sir Simon and William leaving on their journey and Mrs. Phillips bidding them farewell.

© Novel Units, Inc. All rights reserved

Chapter 11   Pages 108-119

Vocabulary

chided 108	mount 109	lists 109	raucous 110
apparitions 110	rooks 111	cacklings 114	

Predicting and Setting the Stage
Read aloud the first paragraph of Chapter 11. How has the scene changed from the toy castle in the Lawrence attic? What will happen next?

Discussion Questions
1. What was "companionable silence" as mentioned on page 108? *(cooperative, supportive feeling between two or more silent friends)* When have you experienced "companionable silence"?

2. Why did Sir Simon look sad when he spoke of Moonlight? *(Answers vary. He remembered a happier time before the wizard's curse. Moonlight was a special pet.)*

3. How does the author create the mood of the forest path? *(Pages 110-111, Details of how it looked, discussion of how branches, etc. impacted Sir Simon and William, details of the sounds; the author provided information for various senses—seeing, hearing, feeling.)*

4. What were the "strange apparitions"? *(They were mirages which could lead Sir Simon and William off the path—light, silver water, "Moonlight.")*

5. How did William overcome the sounds of the forest? *(by playing his recorder)*

6. Who greeted William as he left the forest? *(a small boy who told William about the troubles since Alastor took over)*

7. Why did a shiver run down the boy's back? *(The boy was fearful of Alastor's spies.)*

Supplementary Activities
1. Discover what a tournament would have involved in Sir Simon's time. You might refer to *Living in Castle Times* by Robin G. Usborne.

2. Draw a picture of the forest. Consider using crayon with a black wash over the picture.

3. Create the forest's mood with music and animal sounds.

4. "Music soothes the savage beast." How does the saying relate to the book?

5. What apparition would most likely tempt you?

6. On a class chart or bulletin board, display the rules of chivalry. Chart William's progress and how he measures up to the chivalrous standards.

Chapter 12   Pages 120-130

Vocabulary

brackish 121	striding 121	compassionate 122	hoisted 123
stagnant 124	suffice 127	accursed 127	parched 128
haggard 128			

Discussion Questions

1. What was brackish water? *(foul stagnant water)* How was brackish water typical of the area through which William walked at the beginning of Chapter 12? *(The land was parched, unproductive, in a drought, and unpleasant.)* If you were an author, what would you put in a scene you wanted to be unhopeful, not promising? *(Answers vary.)*

2. Why was an apple important in this chapter? *(A wrinkled old man asked William to fetch an apple for him from the top of a tree. It turned out that when the old man took a bite of the apple, he turned into a young healthy man. The wizard's spell had thereby been broken.)*

3. Why are some phrases set in italic type? *(They provided emphasis. In this chapter those phrases were advice and rules given to William. That advice was important in William's quest.)*

4. How did two birds help William? *(They served to distract him from eating the apple as though they knew it held a wizard's spell for him.)*

5. What important things did the apple man provide to William? *(lunch and information on how to defeat the dragon who guarded the gate to the castle)*

6. What was William's attitude toward advice and his quest in this chapter? Look for quotations in the book. (See next page.)

Prediction
Reread the last paragraph of Chapter 12. What does it mean? What will happen next? In small groups, use your imagination to make up "the legend."

Supplementary Activities

1. Add to your cartoon strips of William's quest adventures with panels for this chapter.

2. Devise a 30 second news bite to summarize William's Chapter 12 adventure.

3. Answer these classic newspaper questions for the Chapter 12 adventure:

Who? What? Where? When? Why?

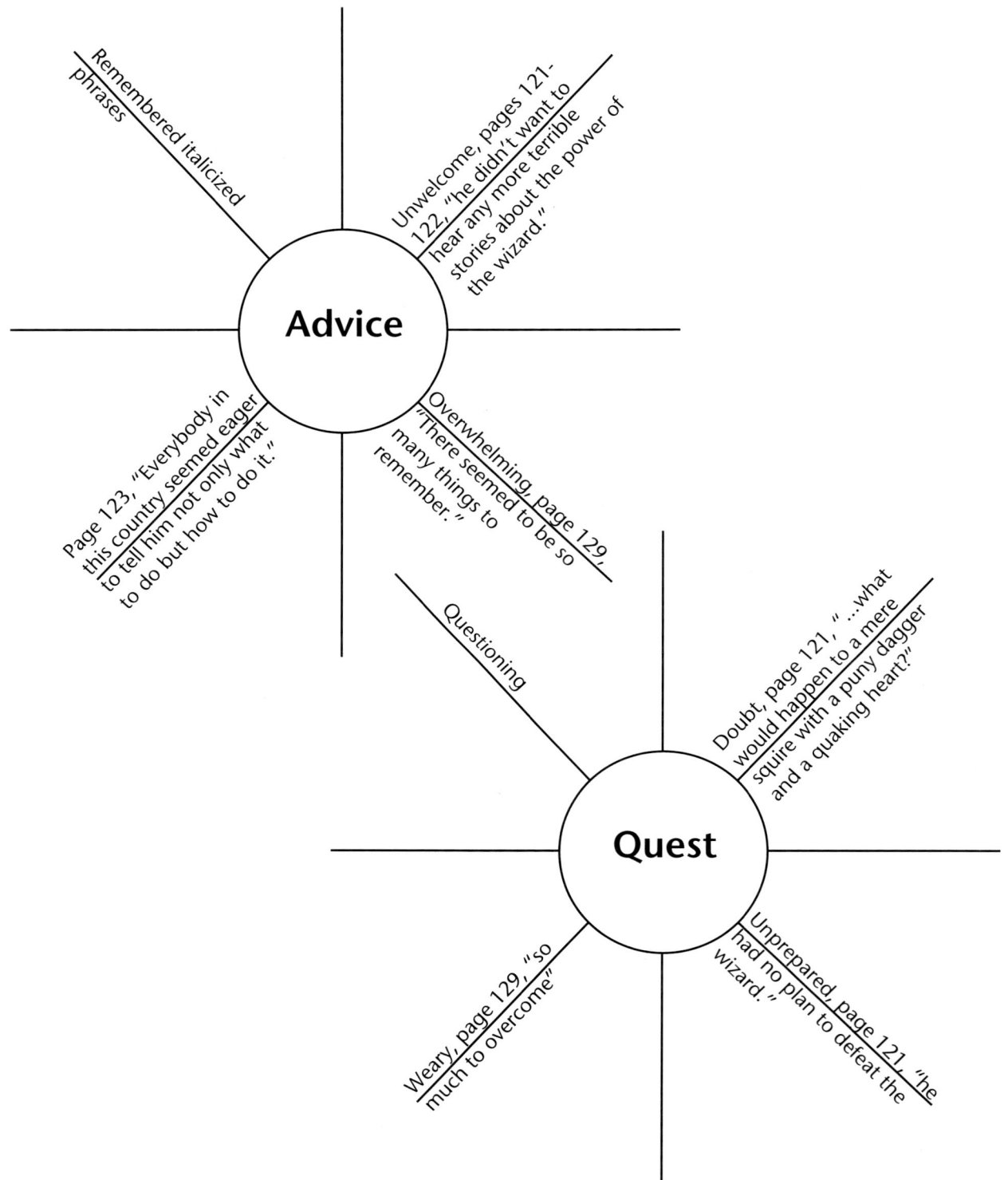

Chapter 13   Pages 131-139

Vocabulary

assent 132	parched 132	battlements 132	prowled 133
withered 133	tapestry 134	tumult 136	anguished 136
falter 136	grotesque 138	ramparts 139	

Discussion Questions

1. How do the villagers react to William? *(with curiosity, give him warnings to turn around)* Why? *(fear for him, hopelessness)*

2. Describe William's first sight of the castle. *(Pages 132-133, "The site had been well chosen, a rocky hill with a path that curled back and forth until it reached the top. A tower stood at each corner, and arrow windows dotted the exterior walls in a random pattern. A single black pennant flew from the corner of one tower.")*

3. Why is there a black pennant flying from one of the towers? *(Answers vary.)*

4. Is William's decision to meet the dragon after a night's sleep a good decision? Why? *(Answers vary. Recall the idea that a knight's greatest strength is in the morning.)*

5. Why does William say, "Oh, please, help me," on page 134? *(He is feeling alone and overwhelmed by his quest.)*

6. Why does William ask Mrs. Phillips which weapon to use? *(Answers vary.)* Can she help him?

7. How does his recorder help William? *(The musical instrument soothes his nerves and gives him a focus as he follows the apple-tree man's directions to defeat the dragon.)*

8. What is the significance of the song William plays on the recorder? *("The Battle Hymn of the Republic" is a war song, is familiar to William, and has a brisk marching tempo.)*

9. Why does William knock three times on the door to the castle? *(Answers vary.)*

Prediction

Will the soldiers keep William's secret? How will the wizard greet William? How will the wizard look?

Supplementary Activities

1. Make a measure of William's confidence when he knocks at the castle door. Use examples from the book as evidence for your answer.

2. What would be the worst illusion you could see in the dragon's eyes? Why?

3. Fill in a story map for the second half of the book starting with William's quest.

Chapter 14   Pages 140-148

Vocabulary
acrid 141	beckoned 141	matted 141	wily 145
lances 146	bide 146	crone 146	

Discussion Questions

1. Where did the "endless spiral of stairs" on page 140 lead? *(They lead to Alastor. It also might be a reference to depths—lower life.)*

2. Draw a picture of Alastor. Does the author's word picture give you enough detail for your drawing?

3. Why would Alastor feel hunted? *(Answers vary. He was evil, and good people sought to defeat him. He <u>was</u> being hunted—by William and earlier by Sir Simon.)*

4. Why might William have considered his gymnastics routine for the wizard a mixed success? *(William concentrated and delivered an excellent routine, but the dagger fell out on the floor and was picked up by Calendar.)*

5. How were William's dilemmas of the dagger and explaining getting past the dragon solved? *(Calendar sniffed the dagger and declared, "no blood." One of the soldiers explained that William had been directed to a side entrance away from the dragon.)*

6. What were the wizard's pets? *(People of the village turned into lead statues.)*

7. Why did William stifle a scream of horror? *(He saw the Silver Knight and the apple-tree man's son turned to lead.)*

8. How did William react when he spotted the object of his quest? *(He remained calm as he mentally considered snatching the medal and trying to escape with it.)*

9. Why do you suppose Sir Simon's frozen expression showed both anger and surprise? *(Answers vary.)*

10. Why do you think William was shown to such an unpleasant, inhospitable room? *(The wizard didn't trust him. The wizard wasn't a good host.)*

11. How was Mrs. Phillips helping William? Or was she helping him? *(Answers vary. She provided a sense of comfort and helped William to find answers within himself.)*

Supplementary Activities

1. Concentration is critical to William in his quest. Consider concentration in your own experiences. Has it been important? How can you increase your concentration? Answer in a short paragraph.

2. Why was William called William as opposed to Bill, Will, Billy, Wils? Discuss and answer in a short paragraph.

3. Draw a cartoon of William at the end of the day in Chapter 14. What thoughts run through his head?

Chapter 15   Pages 149-159

Vocabulary
gyrations 150	churlish 151	scoundrel 151
agonies 152	raspy 153	cowardice 157
ravager 159	etched 159	

Discussion Questions

1. How is the illustration at the beginning of Chapter 15 different from the illustrations in all the chapters before? *(The other half of the medallion is illustrated. This Janus head has a more positive expression and two keys are displayed.)* Why has the illustrator made this change? *(to suggest that William regains the medallion in this chapter)*

2. Why would the wizard be "more eager for an audience than for a fool," as stated on page 149? *(He was lonely. He wanted to brag about his evil exploits.)*

3. Complete an attribute web on Alastor.

4. What did Brian mean when he said, "Hate has no magic in it...We need magic to defeat him"? *(Many people had hated the wizard before but could not defeat him. Magic must be needed.)*

5. Why did the old woman befriend William? *(Answers vary. Perhaps she enjoyed his kind and gentle manner or was lonely herself. She may have shared the secret of the mirror because William told her about the apple-tree man's son.)*

6. How was William's "brain, footwork, and sense of space" (from page 101) crucial in defeating the wizard? *(William distracted the wizard with his routine, used the front somersault to knock the wizard to the ground, grabbed the necklace and moved away, and then used his brain with the mirror.)*

7. Why did William see so little in the mirror? *(He was kind and gentle of spirit.)*

8. Who sent the wizard away? *(Calendar)* Where? *(Answers vary.)*

9. Who destroyed the mirror? *(William)* Why? *(So no one could have such power again.)*

Supplementary Activities

1. Dramatize Chapter 15, perhaps using a Readers Theatre format.

2. Why is seeing inside yourself so frightening? Answer in a short journal entry.

Chapter 16 — Pages 160-171

Vocabulary

tyranny 160	wizened 163	gingerly 164	alchemists 164
baronial 165	tankard 166	Boar's head 167	lulled 167

Discussion Questions

1. What was William's uncertainty at the beginning of Chapter 16? *(how Calendar and the soldiers would react)*

2. What did William have to bring the people back from their leaden state? *(Answers vary—perhaps his gentle, kind nature.)*

3. How did William feel about being addressed as sir? *(Answers vary—perhaps embarrassed, self-conscious.)*

4. What was the fate of Calendar? *(She smiled when Sir Simon accepted her back and declared that she would live with him in comfort, surrounded by her friends.)*

5. Where will Sir Simon keep the lead token so that it will be safe? *(Answers vary.)*

6. Contrast the celebration on page 165 with the scene on page 120 when William was heading for the castle.

Heading to the Castle	Preparing to Leave the Castle
Dusty	Huge banquet table laden with food
Only a few ears of corn	Happy people
Stunted crops	Talkative crowd
Brackish water in dried up streams	
Unhappy people	
Quiet nervous manner	

7. How was William's two-day journey back to the castle and world in the Lawrence attic? *(pleasant, cheering well-wishers along the way, accompanied by Tolliver)*

Supplementary Activities

1. Imagine a festive celebration today. How would it be different from the celebration Sir Simon staged for William? Record on a Venn diagram.

2. Sir Simon said, "...we shall live in each other's thoughts forever." (page 169) What did he mean? Answer in a short paragraph.

3. Dramatize a news conference for William and Sir Simon after defeating the wizard. List questions for reporters and have students play the parts of William and Sir Simon.

Chapter 17 Pages 172-179

Vocabulary

booty 173   cooped 175   eerie 177

Discussion Questions

1. What is different about the illustration at the start of Chapter 17? *(Both parts of the medallion are featured because they will be reunited in this chapter.)*

2. How has William changed because of his quest adventure? *(He is self-confident.)* How has he not changed? *(He physically looks the same.)*

3. What kind of a person lacks imagination? *(Sir Simon and Alfred Phillips who attack problems again and again in the same manner as opposed to trying different approaches.)*

4. How does Mrs. Phillips know that William had defeated the wizard? *(A leaden figure of the wizard has appeared in Mrs. Phillips' room. Calendar had sent the wizard there when she cast a spell.)*

5. What does Mrs. Phillips take with her as a record or memento of her adventures? *(the tapestry)*

6. Why does Mrs. Phillips take the leaden wizard with her? *(So William wouldn't accidentally touch the lead figure and restore it to life.)*

7. Why was restoring William to normal size the last time the magic would work? *(Mrs. Phillips plans to drop both the medallion and the lead wizard into the middle of the Atlantic Ocean.)*

8. Will the token and wizard be safe in the Atlantic Ocean? *(Answers vary.)*

9. Complete the story map to wrap up the story.

Post-reading Activities

1. Compare William in the first part of the story to William at the end. Complete a T-comparison and a Venn diagram to organize your thoughts.

William at the Start	William at the End

2. Design a coat of arms for William. Explain in a short paragraph why it is appropriate. (See page 11 of this guide.)

3. Design a board game of William's quest adventure.

4. Design a t-shirt for William. Explain in a short paragraph why it is appropriate. (See page 12 of this guide.)

5. What is a classic quest adventure?

6. How was the legend told in Sir Simon's kingdom about its rescue from the wizard realized?

Bulletin Board Ideas

1. Diagram enlargement of the castle.

2. Tapestry of the adventure.

3. Chart or web of the weapons (skills) that William uses on his quest.

4. Enlargement of *The Castle in the Attic* board game, designed by students.

5. Code of Conduct (Chivalry) for the Classroom—displayed on a scroll and surrounded by student-designed coats of arms.

Journal Prompts

1. My hands have held...
2. My eyes have seen...
3. My money has gone to...
4. My signature appeared on...
5. My laugh has been heard at...
6. My feet have been...
7. My chivalrous heart has...
8. Explain an English idiom in words.

    | break the ice | walk on eggshells | split hairs |
    | sleep like a log | flipped his lid | in hot water |

9. My imagination...
10. My toy soldier...

Vocabulary Activities

1. Brainstorm synonyms for a commonly-used verb, as in *went* or *ran* or *said*. Then place the words on an expanded web to categorize shades of meaning among the synonyms. (See diagram on next page.)

2. Encourage students to start their personal word bank of words they've learned recently or want to learn. The parallel is to a money bank in which change is saved for use later. Likewise students collect vocabulary words on cards or lists for their personal bank.

3. Students make cards for use in a manila folder board game. On one side of the card, the vocabulary word is used in a sentence. A definition is placed on the reverse side. This pack of the cards provides the "questions" for the game. Alternative boards can also be used, such as Trivial Pursuit or any board game in which players proceed from start to finish through a series of "blocks." Just use the vocabulary cards as the means to proceed.

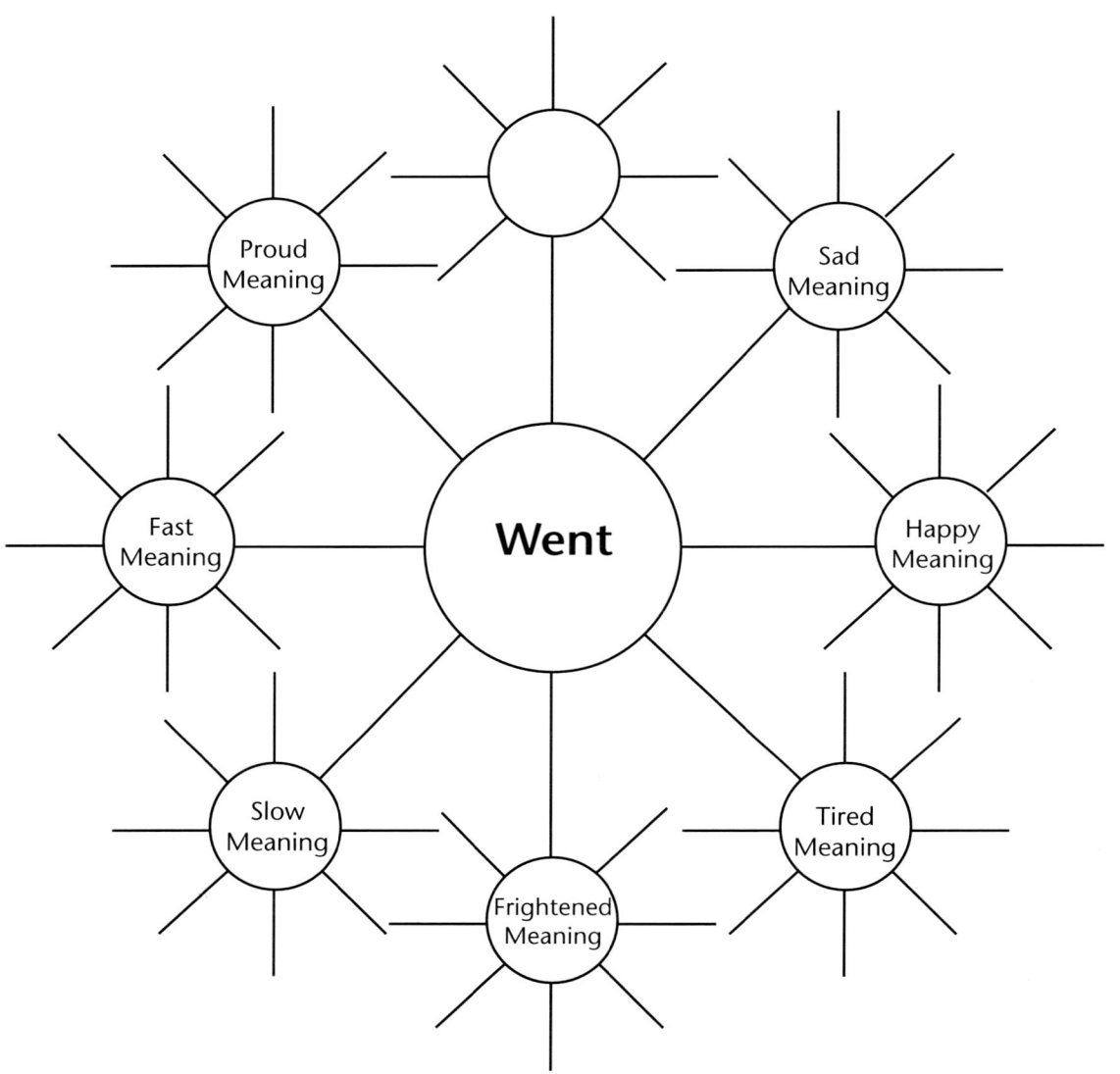

4. Provide a word wall in the classroom where students display on sentence strips (with letters at least four inches high) new words they've learned.

   a) Play "Mind Reader" with teacher choosing a word from the wall. Give successive clues to narrow the choices. All students write down their answer for the game.

   b) Complete a feature matrix using wall words.

5. Thesaurus games finding substitutes for underlined words.
   a) In cartoons
   b) In newspaper articles
   c) In a passage from the book
   d) From a class list of overworked words

6. Make analogies with vocabulary words.

   in—out   hot—

   mother—aunt   father—

   soap—clean   mud—

   Keep a class list of analogy relationships; e.g., opposites, part to whole, whole to part, synonyms.

7. Categorize a group of vocabulary words.

   Possibilities: *structural*

   (Anglo Saxon, Romance, Greek, etc.)

   Topic, function (part of speech), feeling conveyed, formal/informal usage.

8. Develop word maps for selected target vocabulary words. (An example is shown below.)

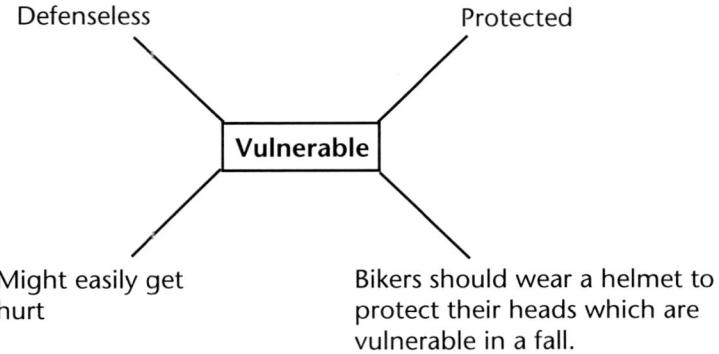

Teacher Background

Janus
A Roman mythological god who had two faces that looked in opposite directions, one looking into the past and one looking into the future. Janus was the god of gates, doors, entrances, and exits. Romans prayed to Janus at the beginning and end of important events, especially wars. The doors to Janus's temple remained open during wars and were closed in peacetime. January was named for Janus.

Saturn
The Roman god of agriculture. The Roman festival honoring Saturn, saturnalia, began on December 17 and lasted a week. The most popular gifts of the celebration were wax candles and small clay figurines.

Castle
The home and fortress of a monarch or noble. Castles were walled fortresses common in Europe from about 400 A.D.—1500 A.D. when feudalism was the political and military system. The monarch's family and servants also lived in the castle. The castle could also be used as a barracks, prison, storehouse, armory, treasure house, and center of local government.

Knights and Knighthood
Knights, warriors equipped and trained to fight on horseback, were part of the feudal system of the Middle Ages. Knights-in-training served as pages from about age seven until age fifteen or sixteen when they became squires. Pages joined the household of another knight or nobleman and learned to handle small weapons and the code of chivalry. A squire was a personal servant to a knight and was trained as a mounted soldier. Any knight could bestow knighthood on another with the words, "I dub you knight." Knighting ceremonies varied in elaborateness.

Gymnastics Terms
Cartwheel:	A spin of the body sidewise, rolling onto the hands and continuing back to the feet. The legs are spread during the maneuver. This creates the effect of spokes on a turning wheel and gives the exercise its name.
Whip:	To throw the arms and legs in a direction to gain force and to aid in accomplishing a trick.
Handspring:	A jump from feet to hands with a thrust to the feet again and with the body moving in one direction.
Round-off:	Also known as Arab spring. This is a version of the cartwheel, but it is completed with the gymnast making a quarter turn from the vertical to land on his/her feet with his/her back to the direction of travel. There is a flight element where the hands and feet are off of the ground.

Bibliography

Non-fiction
Brochard, Philippe. *Castles of the Middle Ages.*
Clark, Richard. *Castles.*
Corbin, Carol. *Knights.*
Fradon, Dana. *Sir Dana: A Knight.*
Gee, Robyn. *Living in Castle Times.*
Goodall, John S. *The Story of a Castle.*
Hindley, Judy. *The Time Traveller Book of Knights and Castles.*
Miquel, Pierre. *The Days of Knights and Castles: 1066-1485.*
Monks, John. *Castles.*
San Soucci, Robert. *Young Merlin.*
Scarry, Huck. *Looking into the Middle Ages.*

Fiction
Chetwin, Grace. *Riddle and the Rune.*
Coville, Bruce. *Jeremy Thatcher, Dragon Hatcher.*
Grahame, Kenneth. *The Reluctant Dragon.*
Graves, Robert. *An Ancient Castle.*
Hamada, Hirosuke. *The Tears of the Dragon.*
Ichikawa, Satomi. *Nora's Castle.*
Landon, Luanda. *Meg Mackintosh and the Mystery at the Medieval Castle.*
Lasker, Joe. *A Tournament of Knights.*
Peet, Bill. *How Droofus the Dragon Lost his Head.*
Rhys, Morgana. *Castle Beneath the Sea.*

Assessment for *The Castle in the Attic*

Assessment is an ongoing process, more than a quiz at the end of the book. Points may be added to show the level of achievement. When an item is completed, the teacher and the student check it.

Name _____ Date _____

<u>Student</u>	<u>Teacher</u>		
_____	_____	1.	Compare William at the start of the story and at the end.
_____	_____	2.	Define a classic quest adventure.
_____	_____	3.	Summarize the story. Use either a story map, a board game, or a multi-panel illustration.
_____	_____	4.	Submit fifteen new vocabulary words learned from the book.
_____	_____	5.	Compare two of the minor characters in the book.
_____	_____	6.	Submit three bits of writing completed in response to the novel.
_____	_____	7.	Write a letter to the principal praising or panning the book.
_____	_____	8.	Complete four vocabulary activities.
_____	_____	9.	Submit a web of ideas filled in response to the novel.
_____	_____	10.	Write a ten item true-false test for classmates to check for reading the book.

Comments: